monday morning®

SCIENCE BOOSTERS

By Dana McMillan and Sidney Martin

Illustrated by Corbin Hillam

Publisher: Roberta Suid
Editor: Mary McClellan
Cover design: David Hale
Design and production: Susan Pinkerton

monday morning®

Monday Morning is a registered trademark of
Monday Morning Books, Inc.

ISBN 0-912107-82-0

Printed in the United States of America
9 8 7 6 5 4 3 2 1

Contents

Introduction

Science is fascinating to children but often intimidating to parents and teachers. Many adults think that teaching science requires expensive equipment, complicated experiments, and expert knowledge. Our goal with *Science Boosters* is to help change that idea.

Science Boosters is a collection of easy-to-make science projects that don't require any special equipment. The directions are simple to follow, and most of the materials can be found in the average home.

Moreover, the activities in *Science Boosters* don't require that adults have all of the answers. In fact, more learning can often take place if the adult and child are learning together in an experimental atmosphere. Many of these projects don't have set solutions. Instead they are open-ended, encouraging the children to learn about science by manipulating a variety of materials and observing the outcome. After constructing a lightning calculator, for example, children can then use it to learn about the movement of sound waves, by measuring the distance of a storm. The concept of sound waves is then made real to them.

Science Boosters is grouped in four chapters to help you choose projects appropriate for your group. The first chapter, Recording and Measuring, gives the children practice in using the scientific process and recording collected information. After making their own science logs, children can then record what they have observed and learned in other science activities.

We hope these activities help you and your children to experience the delight of scientific discovery in everyday things.

Dana McMillan
Sidney Martin
The Learning Exchange
2720 Walnut
Kansas City, MO 64108

RECORDING AND MEASURING

Science Log

Keep records of science projects the way professional scientists do.

MATERIALS:
Notebook with paper
Markers, stickers, or magazine pictures
Pencil

CONSTRUCTION:
1. Decorate the front of the notebook, using markers, stickers, or pictures from magazines. Include the date the notebook was started.
2. Choose a project or experiment in which changes are observed, such as Spicy Sprouts.

USE:
Date each entry in the notebook. Choose the best ways to record procedures and observations. For example: written descriptions, measurements, charts or graphs, light and temperature conditions, drawings, and maps.

Science Categories

This game for two tests science knowledge.

MATERIALS:
Index cards
Marker
Three-minute egg timer

CONSTRUCTION:
1. Print the following categories on cards:

Things found in soil	Things found in the ocean
Things found in ponds	Things found in the desert
Things found in trees	Things found in the mountains
Things found in the sky	Things found on islands

2. Place all of the cards facedown in a pile. Set the egg timer where both players can see it.

USE:
1. The object of the game is for each player to help the other name the category within the time limit.
2. The first player draws a card from the deck and reads the category silently.
3. The first player then turns over the timer and begins giving clues that will help the second player name the category. Clues should not include any words on the card. For example, clues for "things found in soil" could be *earthworms, roots,* and *seeds.*
4. When the time limit is reached, the players switch roles.
5. Keep track of the number of categories each player guesses within the time limit.

VARIATION:
Add new categories to the game.

Clip-a-Temp Gauge

Compare the differences between Fahrenheit and celsius temperatures with this activity.

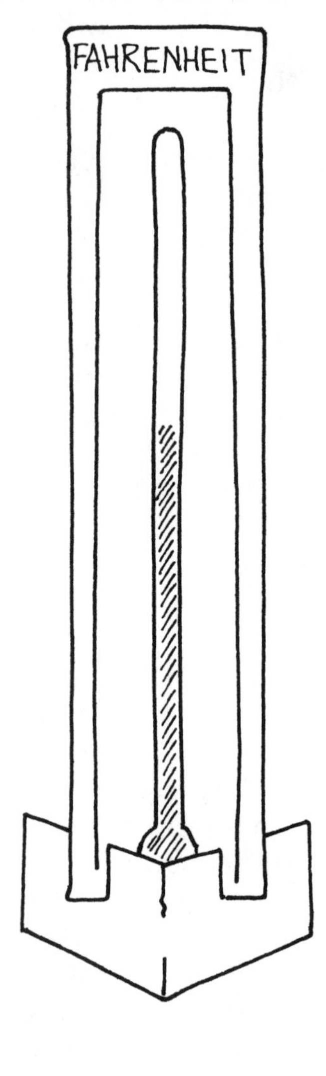

MATERIALS:
White tracing paper
Pencil
Scissors
Sturdy cardboard
Fine-tipped marker
Clothespins (spring-style)

CONSTRUCTION:
1. Trace the two thermometers on the next page onto the tracing paper, and cut them out.
2. Cut a strip of cardboard as wide as one thermometer. Cut the strip long enough to allow space at the top and the bottom.
3. Glue a thermometer to each side of the cardboard strip, making sure the bottom numbers are even with each other.
4. Cut a second strip of cardboard for the base. Fold the strip, and cut slits in it. Insert the thermometer strip in the slits.
5. Use a fine-tipped marker to print these words on the clothespins:

swim day	snow day
coldest day	hottest day

USE:
1. Two players sit opposite each other, with the Clip-a-Temp Gauge between them.
2. Players take turns clipping a clothespin on the thermometer facing them, placing each clothespin where they think it should go. The other player tells the corresponding temperature on the other thermometer. For example, one player clips the "hottest day" clothespin on 45 degrees celsius. The other player responds with "110 degrees Fahrenheit."

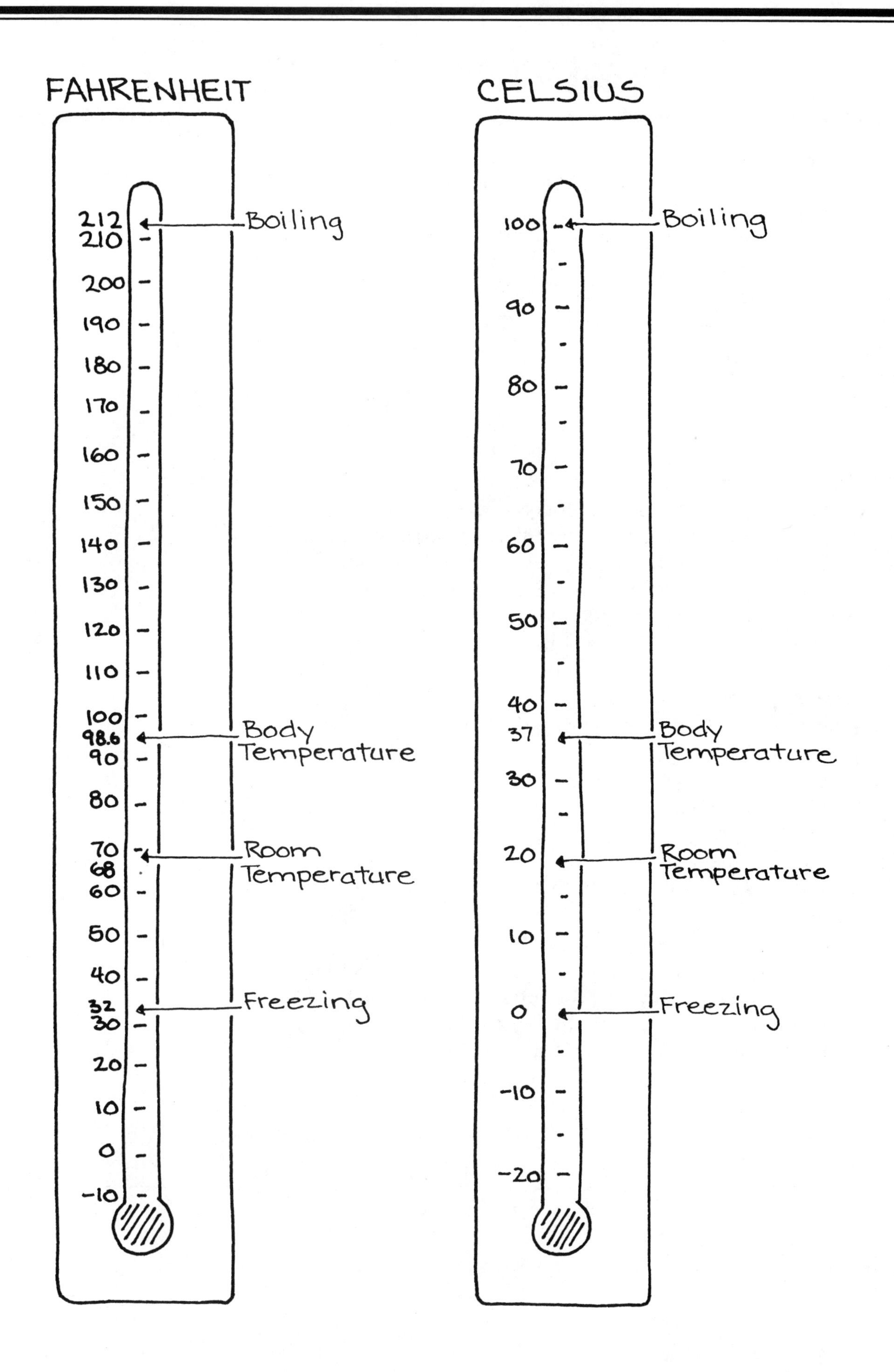
FAHRENHEIT
CELSIUS
212
210
200
190
180
170
160
150
140
130
120
110
100
98.6
90
80
70
68
60
50
40
32
30
20
10
0
-10
Boiling
Body Temperature
Room Temperature
Freezing
100
90
80
70
60
50
40
37
30
20
10
0
-10
-20
Boiling
Body Temperature
Room Temperature
Freezing

Spring Scale

Create a scale to compare the weights of different objects.

MATERIALS:
Oats box
Scissors or knife
Cup hook
Rubber band
Four paper clips
Plastic lid
String

CONSTRUCTION:
1. Cut a window from one side of the oats box.
2. Screw the cup hook into the top of the oats box. Attach the rubber band to the hook.
3. Open each paper clip to form an S-shape. Hook the end of one paper clip over the rubber band.
4. Cut three evenly spaced holes at the edge of the plastic lid. Hook a paper clip through each hole.
5. Tie the three paper-clip ends together with string. Then tie the other end of the string to the fourth paper clip.

USE:
1. Find a food item that has the weight marked on the package. Weigh it on the spring scale. Mark the oats box to show the level of the lid for that weight.
2. Gather several items that seem to be the same weight as the first. Place each on the lid, and see how it compares to the known weight.
3. To mark more weight levels on the scale, find objects that weigh one-half and one-fourth as much as the first object. Mark the oats box to show the level of the lid at these weights.
4. Challenge a friend to find objects that are similar in weight to those marked.

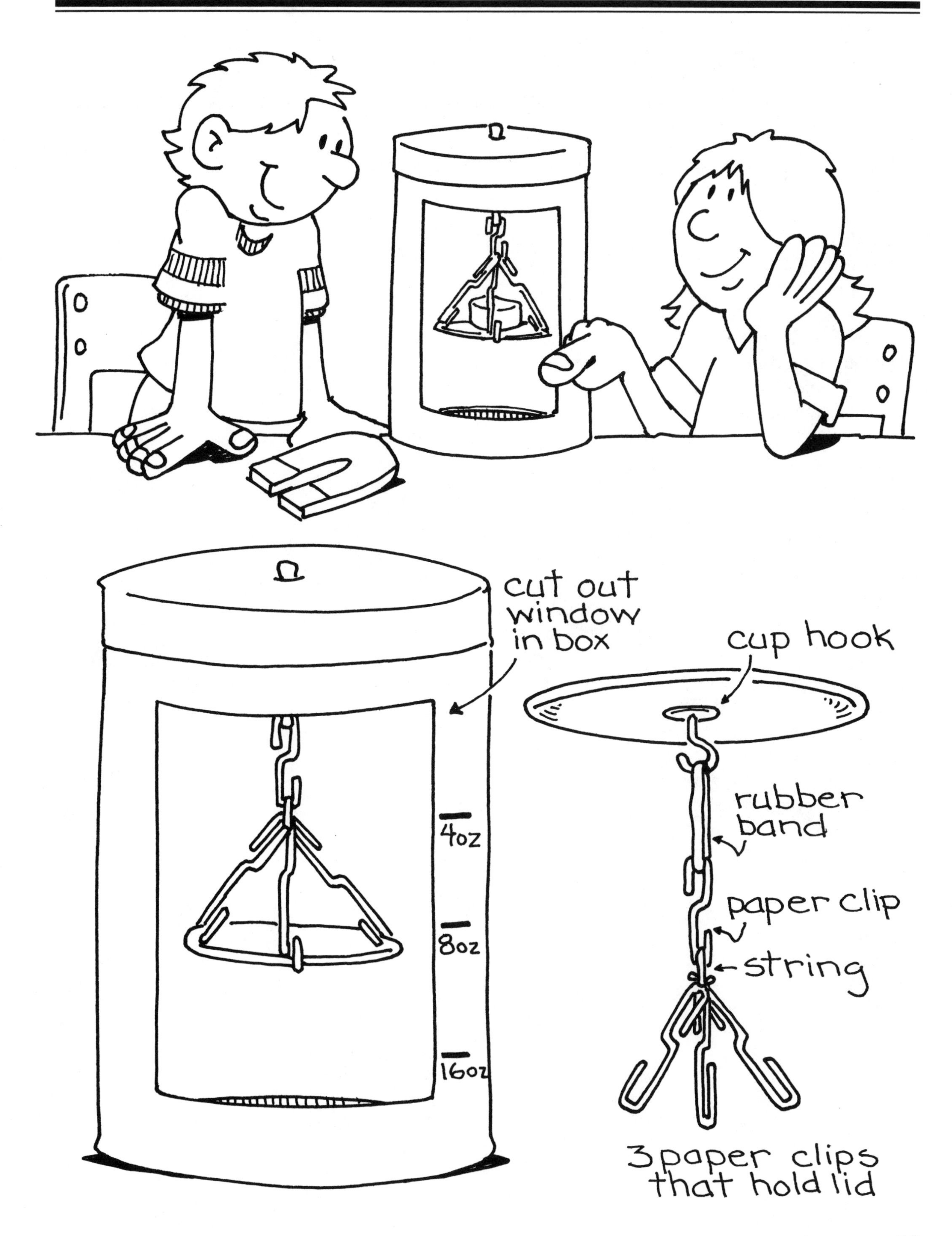
cut out window in box
cup hook
4oz
8oz
16oz
rubber band
paper clip
string
3 paper clips that hold lid

Spider Graphing Game

A spider web provides the perfect grid for this board game.

MATERIALS:
Poster board
Black, red, and green markers
Game pieces

CONSTRUCTION:
1. Use a black marker to draw a spider web on the poster board. (See the Spider Web Pattern.)
2. Mark letters on the "spokes" of the web using a red marker. Mark numbers on the circles in the web with a green marker.

USE:
1. Three or more people can play. The first player chooses a location for the spider on the web, writing down the letter and number without showing it to the others. The player then challenges the other players to find the spider's location.
2. The next player guesses a location on the web, placing his or her game piece there and saying the letter and number.
3. The first player indicates whether or not the guess is correct.
4. If the guess is incorrect, the next player takes a turn.
5. After the first round, if no one has guessed the correct location, the players can then move their pieces to an adjoining spot, over one spoke or circle.
6. The first player to move to the spider's location wins and gets to pick the spider's secret location for the next game.

Spider Web Pattern

Perpetual Calendar

Make a calendar that will work for every year.

MATERIALS:
Oaktag
Drawing compass
Pencil
Scissors
Markers (three different colors)
Hole punch
Brad

CONSTRUCTION:
1. Use the compass to draw three different-sized circles on the oaktag. Cut them out.
2. Use one marker to print the names of the months around the edge of the largest circle. (Divide the circle into 12 equal sections to determine the spacing between months.) Punch a hole above each month.
3. Write 1 through 31 in another color around the edge of the middle-sized circle.
4. Around the edge of the smallest circle, print the names of the days of the week in the third color.
5. Cut the indicator arm from the remaining oaktag. Its length should be a little more than half the diameter of the largest circle.
6. Mark and punch the hole in the indicator arm where it will be attached to the center of the circles. Cut a window large enough for the month and numeral to show. Cut a second window to reveal the day of the week.
7. Stack the three circles so that the center holes made by the compass are lined up. Place the indicator arm on top, and fasten the arm to the circles with a brad.

USE:
1. Set the calendar to show the month, date, and day of the week.
2. Rotate the circles each day to show the new date.
3. Use the hole above each month to hang the calendar.

Let's do lunch sometime.
I'll check my calendar.
JANUARY
1
MONDAY
FEBRUARY
MARCH
APRIL
MAY
JUNE
JULY
AUGUST
SEPTEMBER
OCTOBER
NOVEMBER
DECEMBER
3·4·5·6·7·8·9·10·11·12·13·14·15·16·17·18·19·20·21·22·23·24·25·26·27·28·29·30·31
TUESDAY
WEDNESDAY
THURSDAY
FRIDAY
SATURDAY
SUNDAY

Can and Ladder Clock

Experiment with a new time system by making this unusual clock.

MATERIALS:
Four tin cans (same size)
Nail
Hammer
Step ladder
Water

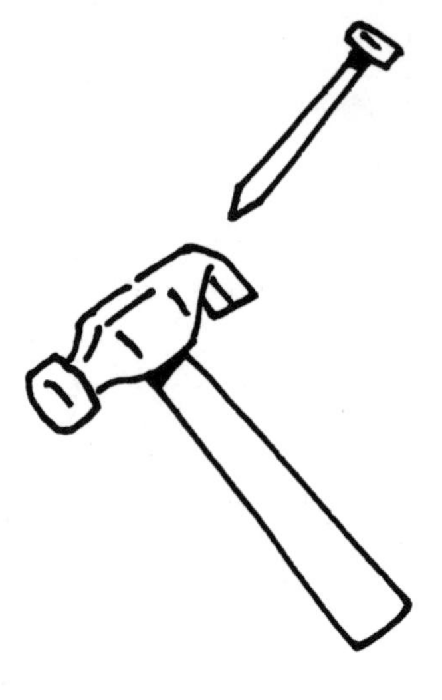

CONSTRUCTION:
1. Wash the cans, removing any labels.
2. Use the nail and hammer to make a small hole near the bottom of three of the cans.
3. Place a can on each step of the ladder. Put the can without a hole on the floor below the others.

USE:
1. Fill the top can with water, and see how much time it takes for all of the water to empty into the bottom can. Change the amount of water until it takes exactly one minute for the cans to empty.
2. Time chores with this clock. Is it possible to feed the dog or make a bed before the clock stops running?
3. Try adjusting the size of the holes to change the speed of the clock. Do larger holes make the water run faster or slower?

Sand Maps

Learn to understand maps that show elevations by modeling mini-landforms in sand.

MATERIALS:
Large cardboard box
Scissors or knife
Trash bag
Sand
Spray water bottle
Colored yarn
Paper
Pencil

CONSTRUCTION:
1. Cut down the box sides to make a large, sturdy tray.
2. Line the inside of the box with the trash bag.
3. Fill the box with sand.
4. Spray the sand with water until it is damp.

USE:
1. Mold the damp sand into a model landscape. Include several different landforms: mountains, hills, canyons, streams, valleys, and lakes.
2. Cut the yarn into a variety of lengths. Knot the ends of each piece together to make loops of various sizes.
3. Find an elevation in the sand model on which to lay each loop so its height will be the same all around. Continue until there is a series of yarn lines at regular intervals on the model.
4. Stand above the model. From this bird's-eye view, draw a map of the model on paper. Draw the yarn loops as contour lines.
5. Flatten the sand in the box. Challenge a friend to re-create the landforms in the sandbox, using the map.

NOTE:
"Topographical maps" show the height of the land. The "contour lines" on the maps represent changes in elevation, usually measured in feet. When contour lines are close together, the slope is steep. When the lines are far apart, the slope is gradual. Topographical maps help us picture how the land looks.

Sorting Machine

Construct a device for separating materials by size.

MATERIALS:

Four boxes (same size)
Utility knife
Tools for making holes (nails, pen, knitting needle, compass, ice pick, large sewing needle)
Tape

CONSTRUCTION:

1. Mark A, B, and C on three boxes. Cut holes in the bottom of box A that are big enough for the dried beans to pass through.
2. Poke holes in the bottom of box B large enough for a rice grain to pass through.
3. Poke holes large enough for a salt grain to pass through in the bottom of box C.
4. Stack the boxes on top of each other: box A on top, B in the middle, and C on the bottom. Place the fourth box below box C. Tape the boxes together.

USE:

1. Put the beans, rice, and salt in box A. Shake the boxes gently until all of the materials have disappeared.
2. Remove the tape, and check the boxes to see where the materials ended up.

VARIATION:

Try sorting other materials: coarse sand and gravel, old buttons, marbles of different sizes, coins, birdseed, breakfast cereals, or popped and unpopped corn kernels. Size the holes in the boxes accordingly.

SIGHT AND SOUND

Mini-Microscope

Use this instrument to magnify tiny things.

MATERIALS:
Large, empty matchbox
Scissors
Aluminum foil
Glue
Nail
Cellophane
Tape
Small glass slide

CONSTRUCTION:
1. Cut away about one-third from the end of the outer box.
2. At one end of the inner box bottom, cut away a one-inch section. At the opposite end, make cuts at the corners, and bend the end flap outward.
3. Cut a small piece of aluminum foil to fit the end flap, and glue it on.
4. Poke a small nail hole in the center of the other end of the inner box.
5. Cut a small piece of cellophane. Place it over the hole, and tape it down at the edges.
6. Insert the inner box into the outer box. Place the glass slide under the hole.

USE:
1. Set the microscope in a place where light can shine on the foil.
2. Place a drop of water on the cellophane, just over the hole.
3. Put a very small object on the glass slide, and center it under the hole. Try examining a tiny insect, a seed, or kitchen spices.
4. Close one eye, and look through the hole. Gently move the inner box up and down to find the best focus. The water drop will magnify the object, and the aluminum foil will reflect the light to show the image clearly.

VARIATION:
A small sheet of clear cellophane, like that used on food and cigarette packages, can be substituted for the glass slide.

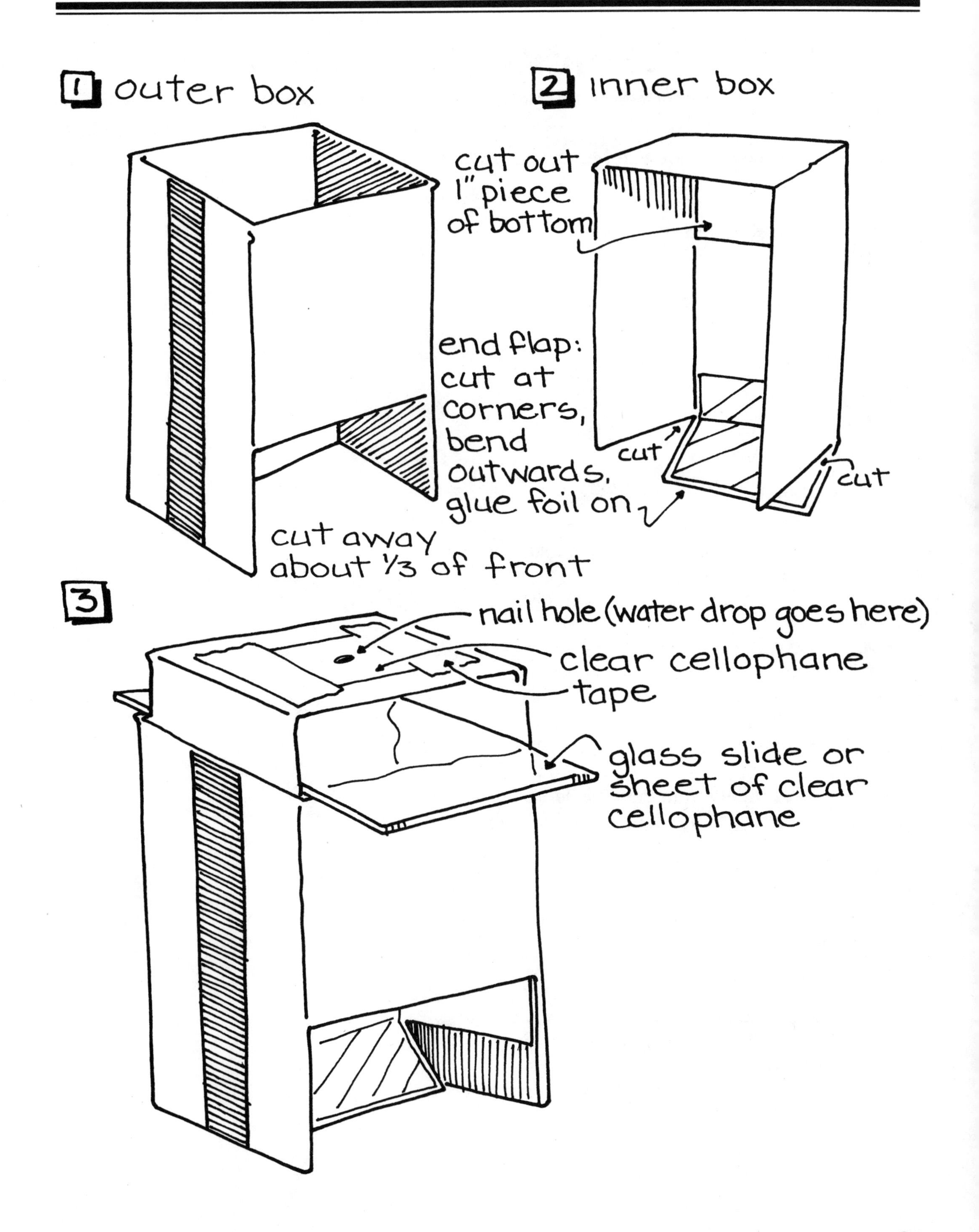

1 outer box
2 inner box
cut out
1" piece
of bottom
end flap:
cut at
corners,
bend
outwards,
glue foil on
cut
cut
cut away
about 1/3 of front
3
nail hole (water drop goes here)
clear cellophane
tape
glass slide or
sheet of clear
cellophane

Kaleidoscope

Make a toy that people have enjoyed for many years.

MATERIALS:
Snack can with lid and silver interior
Scissors or knife
Lightweight cardboard
Mylar or two mirrors
Glue
Styrofoam tray
Tape
Clear plastic
Sequins, glitter, buttons, colored cellophane
Decorative adhesive paper

CONSTRUCTION:
1. Cut the bottom from the can.
2. Cut a sheet of cardboard that, when folded in a V-shape, will fit inside the can.
3. Cover one side of the cardboard with Mylar, or glue on the two mirrors.
4. Fold the cardboard into a V-shape, with the mirrored side facing in. Place the cardboard in the can.
5. Use the can lid as a pattern to cut a circle from the Styrofoam. Cut a hole about the size of a quarter in the center of the circle. Tape the circle to the top of the can to make the eyepiece.
6. Use the lid as a pattern to cut a circle from the clear plastic and a narrow ring from the Styrofoam. Fit the Styrofoam ring inside the lid.
7. Place the small objects in the lid. Place the plastic circle on top, and tape it so that the edges are secure.
8. Tape the lid onto the bottom of the can.
9. Cover the can with decorative paper.

USE:
1. Look through the hole into the can. Face a window or another source of light. The objects will form moving patterns as the can is turned.
2. Shake the can to arrange the objects in a new way.

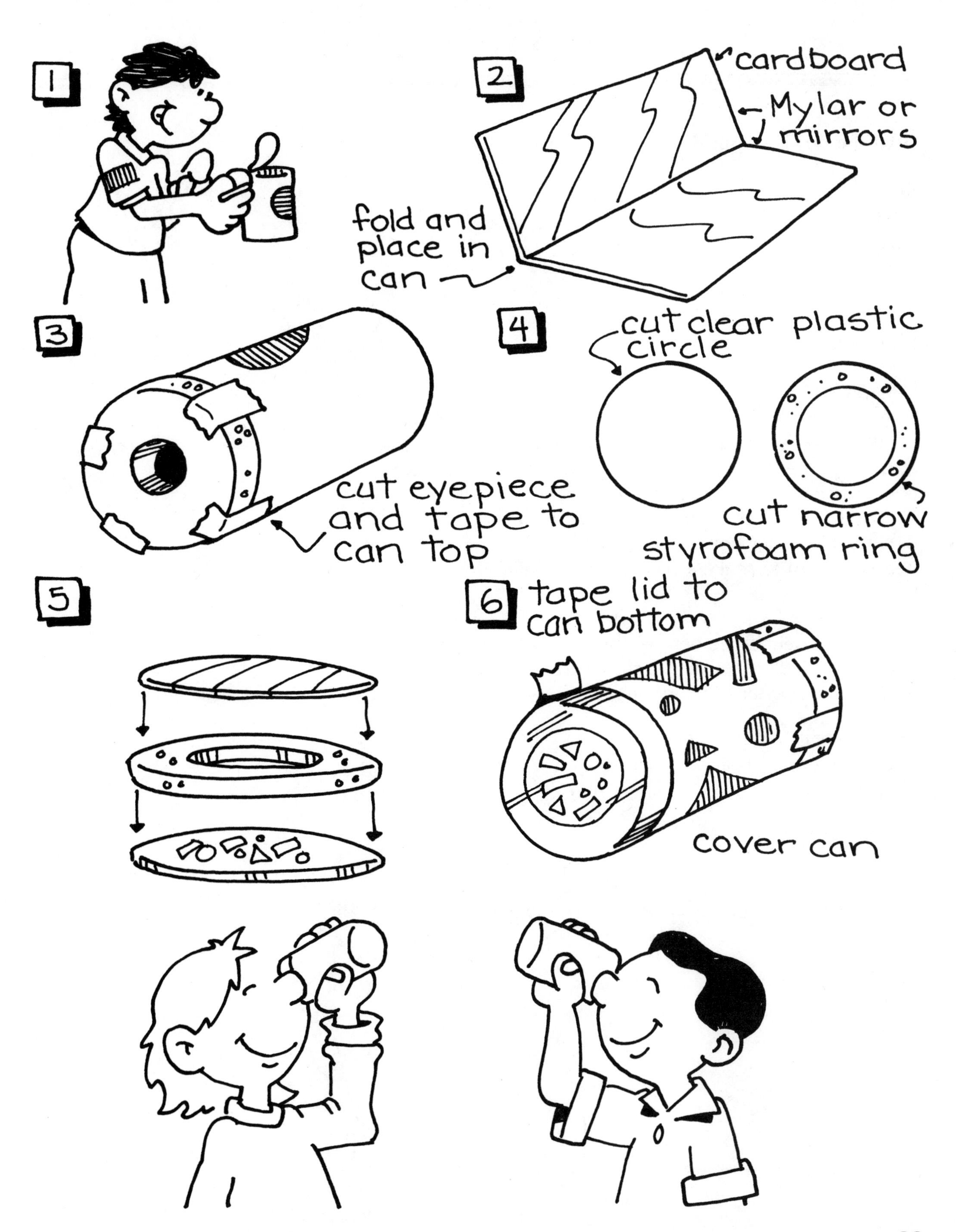
1
2
cardboard
Mylar or mirrors
fold and place in can
3
cut eyepiece and tape to can top
4
cut clear plastic circle
cut narrow styrofoam ring
5
6
tape lid to can bottom
cover can

Nature Thaumatrope

Spin the dowel to put the bird in its nest.

MATERIALS:
White paper
Colored markers or crayons
Scissors
Poster board
Glue
Small wooden dowel

CONSTRUCTION:
1. Trace two circles on the white paper and two circles on the poster board, all the same size, and cut them out.
2. Use the markers or crayons to draw a bird on one of the paper circles and a nest on the other one.
3. Glue the pictures to the poster board circles.
4. Glue the poster board circles back to back, with the dowel between them to make a handle. Let the glue dry.

USE:
Hold the dowel handle between both hands, and rub them back and forth rapidly. This will flip the picture back and forth, making the bird appear to be in the nest.

VARIATION:
Try making other Nature Thaumatropes, such as clouds and a rainbow, a groundhog making its burrow, or leaves appearing on a tree.

1
draw bird on
one circle

2
draw nest on
the other

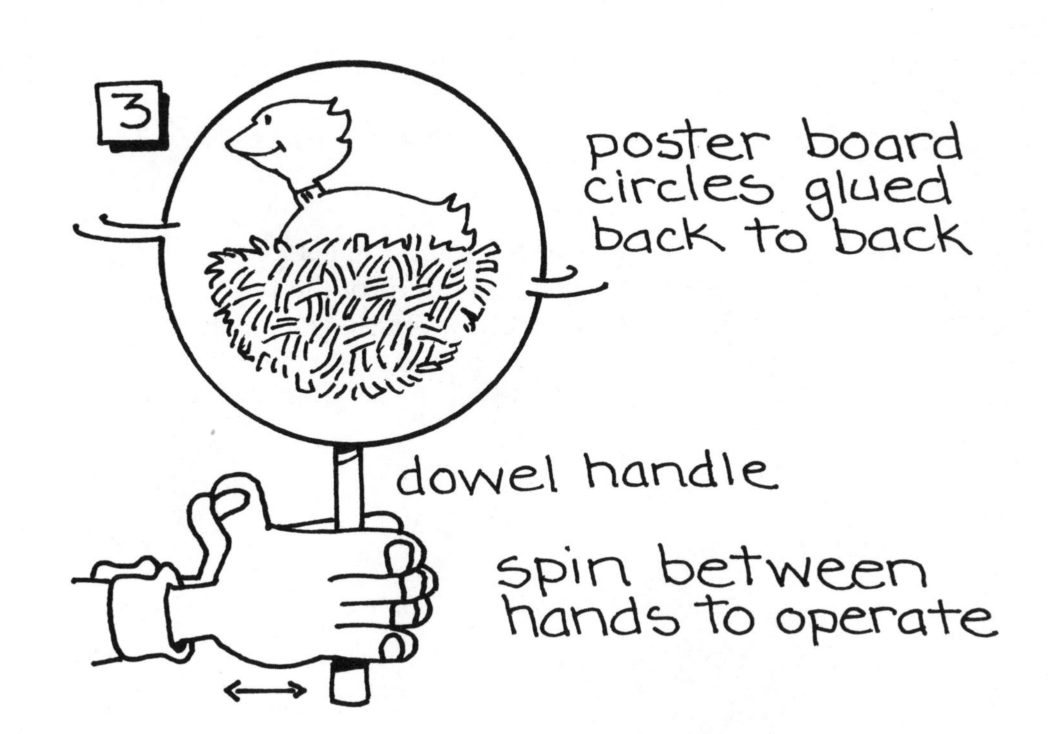
3
poster board
circles glued
back to back
dowel handle
spin between
hands to operate

Star Gazer

Create a galaxy to view day or night.

MATERIALS:
Oats box
Scissors or knife
Thin pieces of cardboard
Pencil
Nail
Flashlight
Tape
Black construction paper
Marker

CONSTRUCTION:
1. Cut out the bottom of the oats box.
2. Cut a piece of cardboard that is bigger than the bottom of the oats box.
3. Find some drawings of constellations, such as the Little Dipper and Leo, in an encyclopedia, and copy them in pencil on the pieces of cardboard.
4. Punch out the constellation patterns with the nail. Make bigger holes for bigger stars.
5. Write the name of the constellation on each cardboard piece.

USE:
1. Tape the black paper on the wall, and turn off the lights.
2. Hold a constellation pattern against the bottom of the box, and shine the flashlight in the other end. The constellation will appear on the black paper.
3. Show the different constellations, and have other people try to guess which ones they are.

Leo

Orion

black paper
cardboard
oatmeal box
flashlight

Ursa Major (Big Dipper)

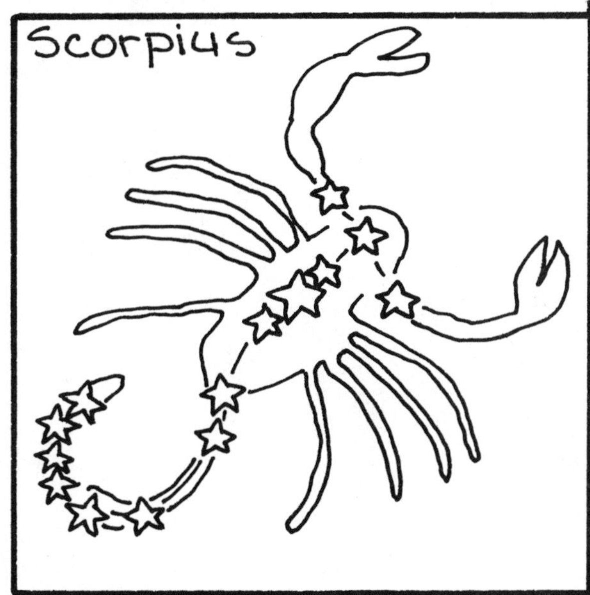
Scorpius

Light Reflectors

Create light patterns on a wall with these cards.

MATERIALS:
Black poster board
Scissors
Aluminum foil
Glue

CONSTRUCTION:
1. Cut the black poster board into small squares.
2. From the aluminum foil, cut shapes that will make interesting patterns.
3. Glue the foil shapes onto the poster board squares.

USE:
1. Hold a card so that it is facing the sun or a bright light bulb.
2. Move the card so that the light reflects off the foil shapes, making patterns on a wall. Jiggle the card to make the patterns move.
3. Hold a card in each hand, making the patterns combine and change as the cards move.
4. Have a group of people hold cards to fill a wall with a pattern collage.

Paper Cup Projector

Make a projector to show original movies.

MATERIALS:
Paper or Styrofoam cup
Scissors or knife
Strip of clear plastic
Fine-tipped permanent marker
Flashlight

CONSTRUCTION:
1. Cut a square hole in the bottom of the cup.
2. Cut a slit in each side of the cup near the bottom. The slits should be wide enough for the plastic strip to slip through.
3. Mark panels on the strip, making them the same size as the hole in the bottom of the cup. Leave a portion of the strip blank on each end.
4. Use the permanent marker to draw a simple scene in each panel. Draw different scenes, or draw pictures that tell a story.

USE:
1. Feed the plastic strip through the slits.
2. Place the flashlight in the cup opening, so that the light will go through the hole in the bottom.
3. Darken the room, and shine the light against a white wall.

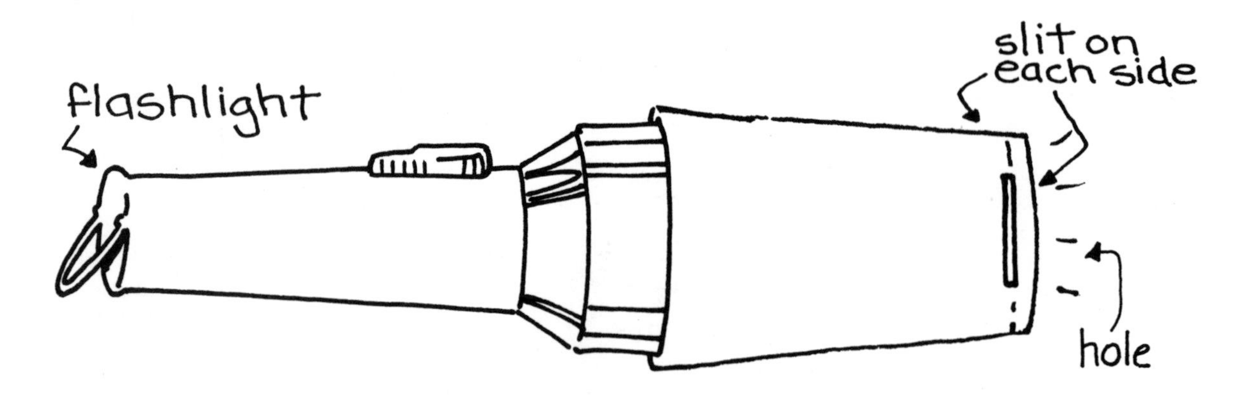

Waterscope

Use this underwater viewer outdoors or in a bathtub.

MATERIALS:
Large tin can
Can opener
Clear plastic wrap
Rubber band

CONSTRUCTION:
1. Use a can opener to cut the bottom from the can. Make sure all the edges are smooth.
2. Cut a sheet of plastic wrap larger than the can opening. Place it over one end of the can, and secure it with the rubber band, pulling the plastic tight.

USE:
1. To use the Waterscope, dip the plastic-covered end into the water, and peer through the open end. Underwater objects will be seen more clearly, because the Waterscope eliminates surface reflections. Objects will also appear somewhat magnified by the water.
2. Use the Waterscope in the bathtub to examine toes or bath toys.
3. Visit a small stream or pond, and examine it with the Waterscope.
4. Collect pond or lake water in a plasic dish pan. Use the Waterscope to examine crayfish, tadpoles, or other creatures in the water.

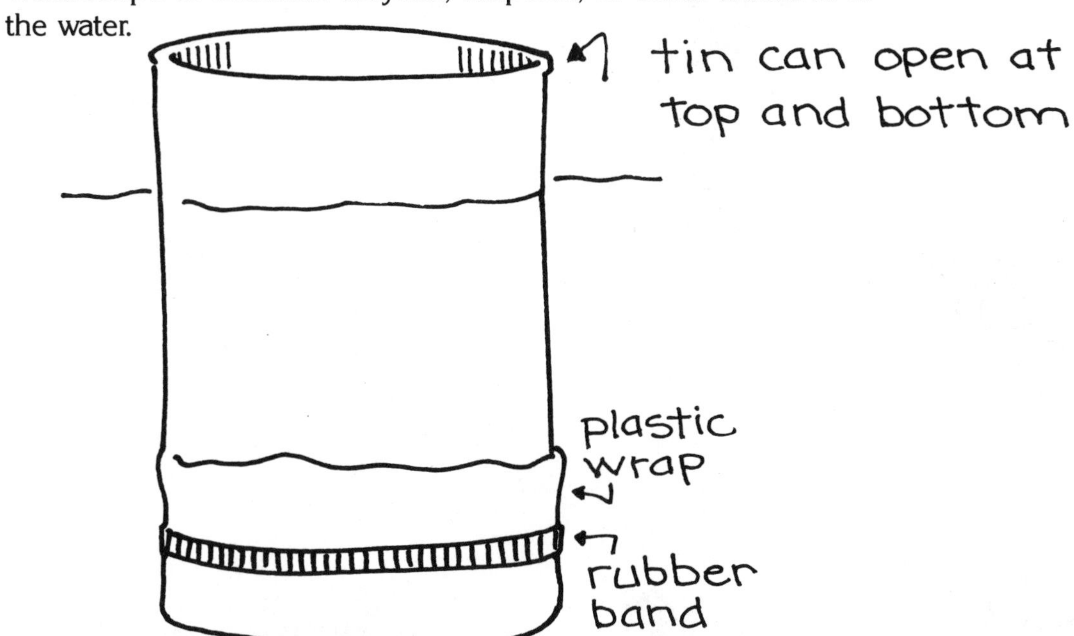

Tube Telephone

Hook up a telephone to talk to a friend.

MATERIALS:
Two clean plastic bottles
Scissors or knife
Garden hose section
Tape

CONSTRUCTION:
1. Cut the tops from the plastic bottles, discarding the bottoms.
2. Fit a top into each end of the hole, and secure it with tape.

USE:
1. Ask a friend to help test the Tube Telephone. Stand as far apart as the hose section permits.
2. Speak slowly and distinctly into one end of the telephone, while the other person listens on the other end.
3. Use a code to signal that a person is finished speaking. For example, say "Go" or "Over" to signal that the other person may begin. Say "Out" when the conversation is over.

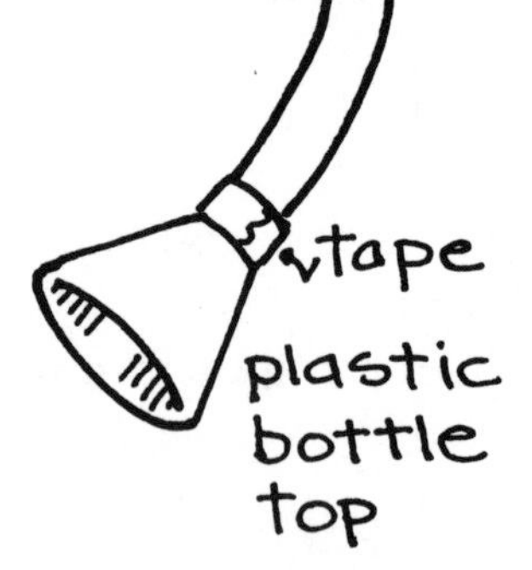

VARIATIONS:
1. Experiment with various sizes and shapes of plastic bottles to improve the sound.
2. Convert the Tube Telephone to a stethoscope by removing one of the plastic bottle tops. Place the remaining bottle top against the chest, and listen through the other end of the hose.

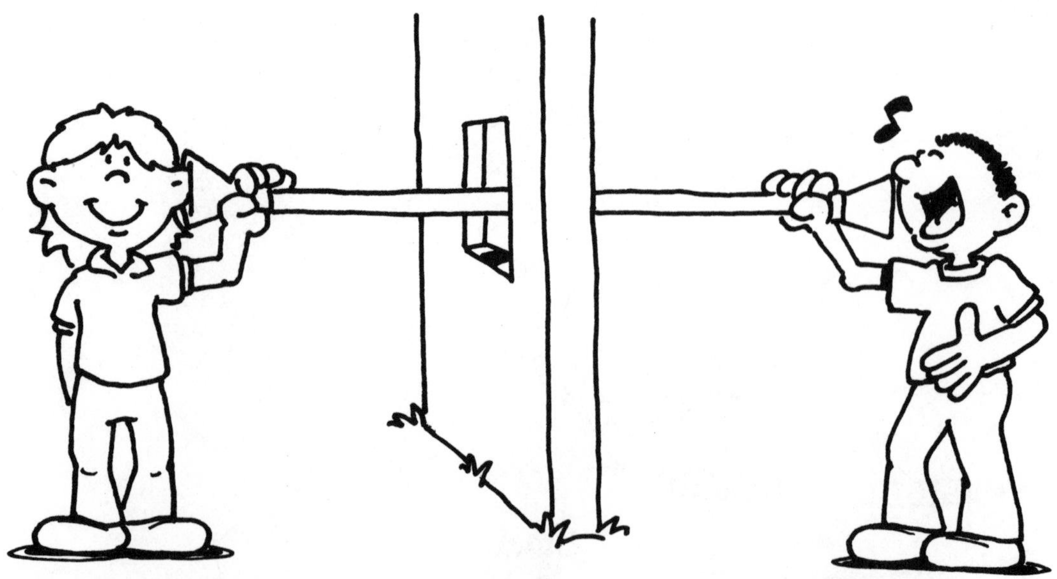

Sound Machine

Use this invention to "see" voices.

MATERIALS:
Tin can
Can opener
Balloon
Scissors
Large rubber band
Small piece of mirror
Glue

CONSTRUCTION:
1. Remove both ends of the can. Be sure that there are no sharp edges left on the can.
2. Stretch the balloon by blowing it up several times. Cut a large section from the balloon.
3. Stretch the balloon section over one end of the can, using the rubber band to hold it in place.
4. Glue the small piece of mirror onto the balloon, slightly off-center.

USE:
1. Use a sunny room that has a shaded wall next to the window.
2. Hold the can so that the sunlight is reflected from the mirror onto the wall.
3. Speak into the open end of the can. Watch the reflection on the wall move. Try speaking in a lower-pitched voice and then a higher-pitched one. Does the reflection on the wall change?
4. Have someone else speak into the sound machine. Watch the reflection. Try singing into the sound machine and notice how the light moves.

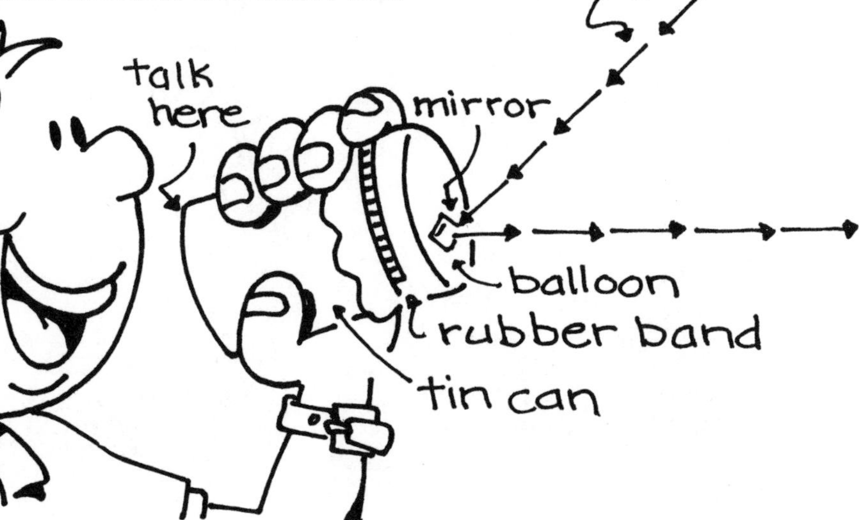

Number Sounds

Use sounds to put the jars in numerical order.

MATERIALS:
Ten babyfood jars
Marbles
Permanent marker
Masking tape

CONSTRUCTION:
1. Place one marble in the first jar, two in the second, and so on, until the last jar has ten marbles in it.
2. On the bottom of each jar, write the number of marbles it contains.
3. Seal the jars with masking tape.

USE:
1. Mix up the jars so that they are not in numerical order.
2. Blindfold a friend. Have that person gently shake each jar, guess how many marbles are in it, and place the jars in numerical order.
3. Remove the blindfold. Check the numbers on the jar bottoms to see whether or not the jars are in the correct order.

VARIATION:
Substitute dried beans for the marbles. Are they easier or harder to put in numerical order?

WEATHER AND ENERGY

Hailstone Gauge

Use this device to measure the size of hailstones.

MATERIALS:
Styrofoam egg carton
Utility knife
Ruler
Permanent marker
Small plastic bags

CONSTRUCTION:
1. Cut the lid from the egg carton.
2. Using the ruler, mark the lengths along the edge of the lid. Convert the measurements to metric, if preferred.
3. Cut the slots with the utility knife, leaving a small distance between slots.
4. Cut the egg cups apart so that each cup is separate.

USE:
1. Use an egg cup to scoop a hailstone into the lid. Avoid touching the hailstones with your hands.
2. Roll the hailstone along the slotted edge of the lid, and find the slot that is closest in size to the hailstone.
3. Place the hailstone back in the egg cup, and record its measurement on the cup with the marker. What was the average size of the hailstones produced by the storm?
4. To save the hailstones, cover each cup with a small plastic bag, and store it in the freezer.

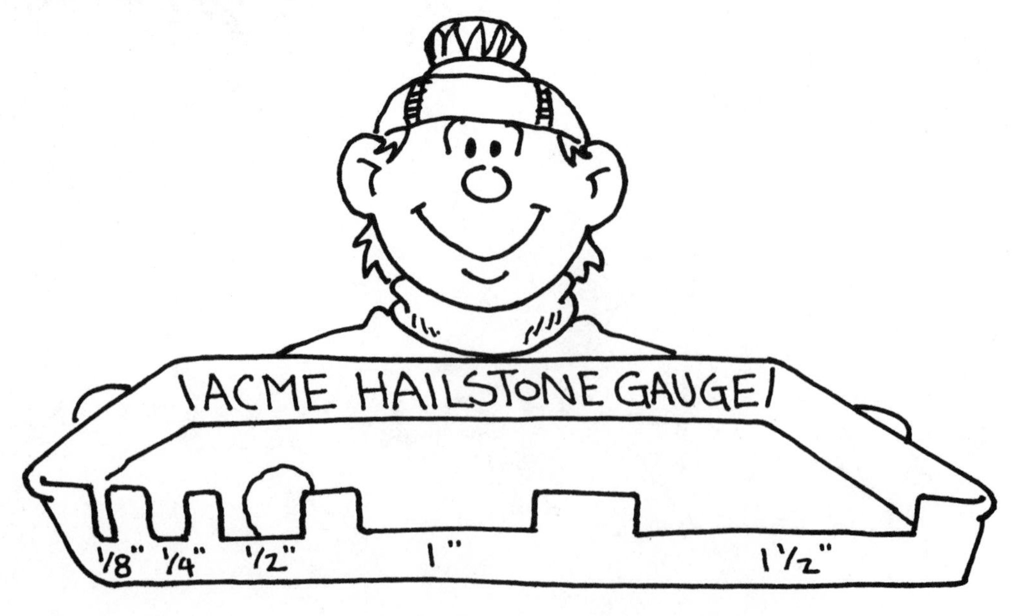

Rain or Snow Gauge

Measure the amount of rainfall or snowfall with this device.

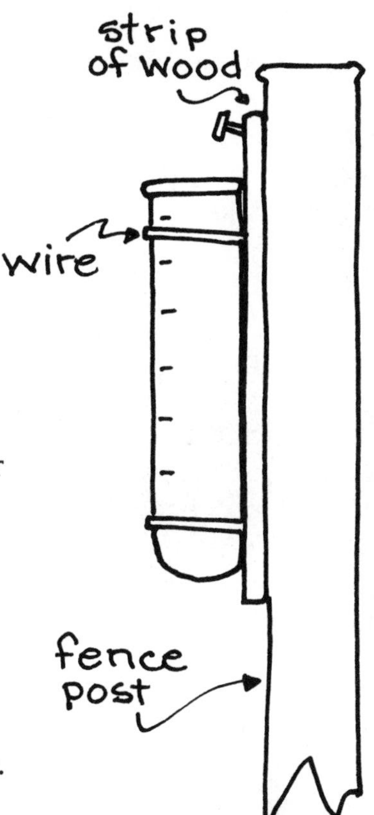

MATERIALS:
Narrow jar with straight sides (such as an olive jar)
Ruler
Permanent marker
Two long wire ties (such as celery ties)
Wood strip
Nails or wire

CONSTRUCTION:
1. Beginning at the bottom of the jar, use the ruler and marker to mark and label inches and quarter-inches.
2. Wire the jar to the strip of wood, leaving the wire loose enough so that the jar can be removed easily.
3. Nail or wire the wood strip to a fence post or other support outdoors where it can collect rain or snow.

USE:
1. After a storm, check the level of water or snow in the gauge.
2. Be sure to empty the jar after each reading.
3. Record the amount in a Science Log.
4. Compare the recordings with newspaper or television weather reports. Remember that rainfall and snowfall can vary even within the same town.

Nephoscope

Keep an eye on the clouds with this weather instrument.

MATERIALS:
Cardboard pizza wheel (10 or 12 inches in diameter)
Crayons or markers
Ruler
Small mirror
Glue
Directional compass

CONSTRUCTION:
1. Draw lines on the circle to indicate the directions of a compass. Label the directions: N = north, E = east, S = south, W = west. Add more specific directions: NE = northeast, NW = northwest, SE = southeast, SW = southwest.
2. Glue the mirror in the center of the cardboard.

USE:
1. When there are clouds in the sky, take the Nephoscope outside and lay it on a flat surface.
2. Use the directional compass to determine which direction is north. Turn the Nephoscope so that the side marked N is facing north.
3. As a cloud passes over the mirror, note the direction from which it enters the mirror and the direction in which it leaves the mirror.
4. Write the observations in a Science Log. Use an arrow to show the movement (for example, S → N). This is the wind direction at cloud height.
5. Keep a record of the movement of clouds for a week. Which direction do the clouds come from most often? Read or listen to weather reports to see which direction the wind will be blowing the following day. Use the Weather Forecasting Chart and the Nephoscope to see if the weather predictions are correct.

Weather Forecasting Chart

Wind Blowing From	Forecast
North	Cold
Northeast	Rain or snow
East	Rain
Southeast	Rain or snow
South	Warm
Southwest	Fair
West	Fair
Northwest	Fair

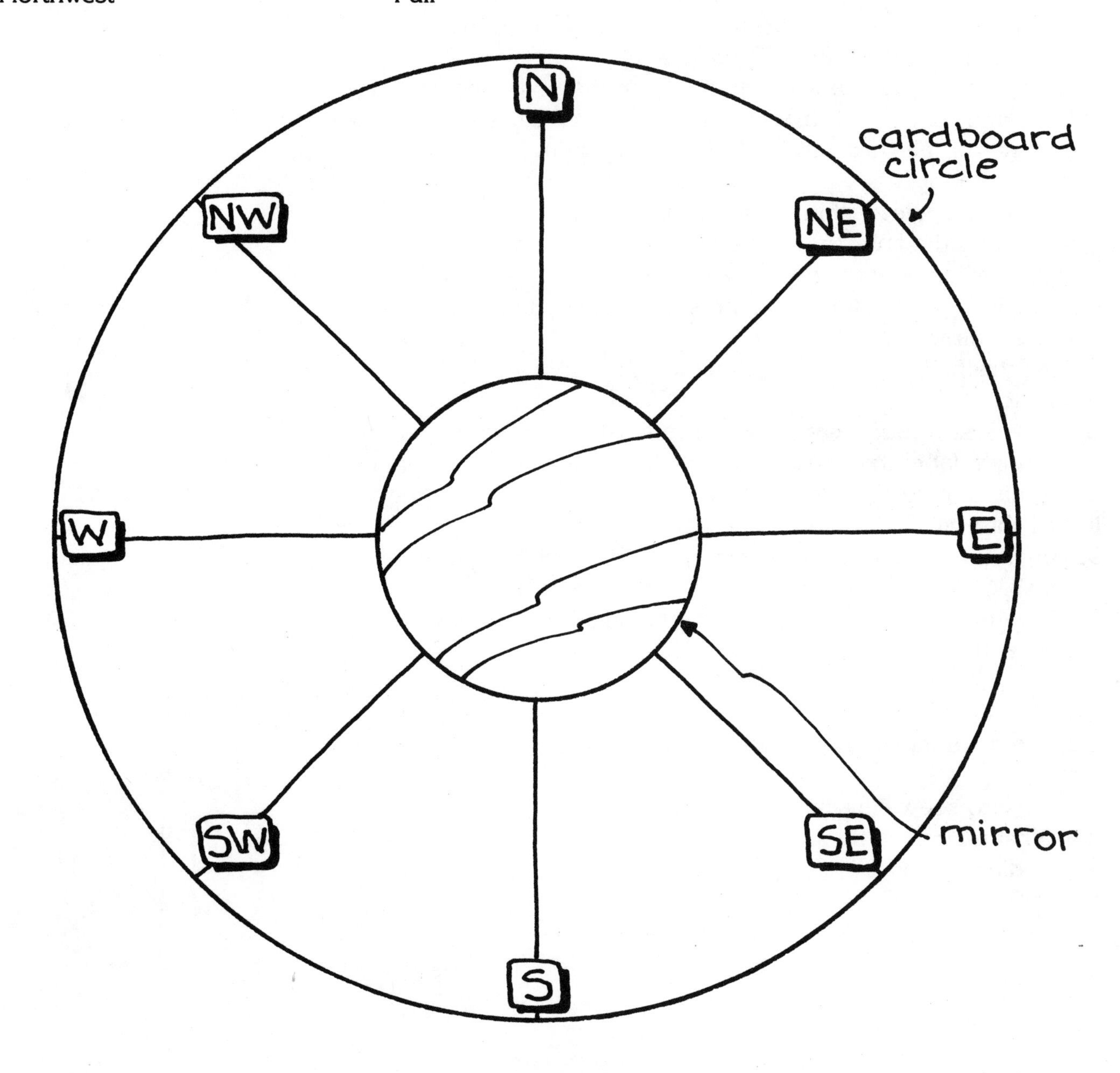

Sundial

Shadows cast by the sun operate this clock.

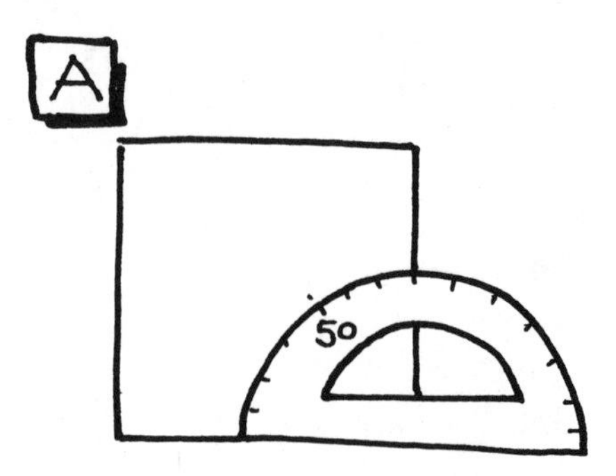

MATERIALS:
Poster board
Protractor
Pen or marker
Popsicle stick

CONSTRUCTION:
1. Check an atlas or call the library to find the latitude for your area. Subtract that latitude from 90 degrees. (For example, 40 degrees from 90 degrees = 50 degrees.)
2. Use the protractor to mark an angle on the poster board that is the same number of degrees as your answer. Draw a line from the corner of the board through the mark. Then draw lines to form a rectangle.
3. Label the angles within the rectangle.
4. Cut along the lines to make two triangles.
5. Cut a rectangle from the remaing posterboard.
6. Center the protractor on a long side of the rectangle, and outline the protractor's outer edge.
7. Mark each 15-degree interval around the outer edge of the protractor.
8. Draw lines through each mark, and label them. Starting at the bottom-left, label the lines 6 through 12. (The line in the middle of the dial will be 12.) On the right side, after the 12, label the lines 1 through 6.
9. Punch a hole where the lines meet on the dial face, and poke a Popsicle stick through the hole at a 90-degree angle.
10. Glue the triangles to the back of the sundial with the labeled angles at the top.

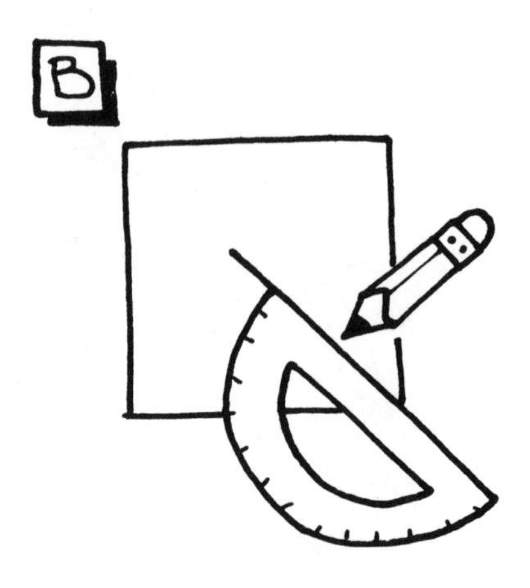

USE:
1. Place the sundial on level ground in a sunny place, facing north.
2. Check to see where the shadow falls on the dial. Then check it against a clock. If there's a difference, make sure the sundial is facing directly north. How will daylight saving time affect the sundial's accuracy?

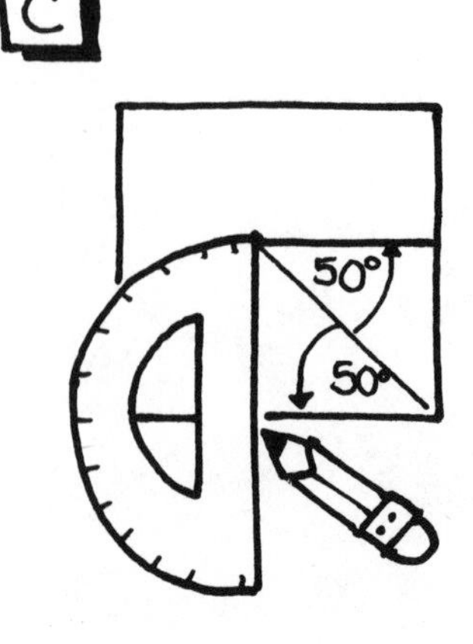

this angle= 90° minus latitude
15° intervals
6
7
8
9
10
11
12
1
2
3
4
5
6
face north

Sand Pendulum

Create geometric designs with this unique art tool.

MATERIALS:
Plastic funnel
Scissors
String
Two cup hooks
Black paper
Sand
Food coloring
Babyfood jar

CONSTRUCTION:
1. Poke three holes in the mouth of the funnel.
2. Tie equal lengths of string through the holes. Tie the ends together at the top.
3. Screw a cup hook in each side of a doorway, inside the frame.
4. Tie a string from one hook to the other. Tie another string in the center of the other string. Make sure that the second string will hold the funnel just off the floor.
5. Place the black paper on the floor below the string.

USE:
1. Fill the funnel with sand, holding a finger under the spout.
2. To create sand designs on the paper, let go of the funnel and let it swing gently back and forth.
3. Color some sand by placing it in a babyfood jar, along with some food coloring. Shake the jar to distribute the color. Add one color of sand at a time to the funnel, and create a multi-colored design.

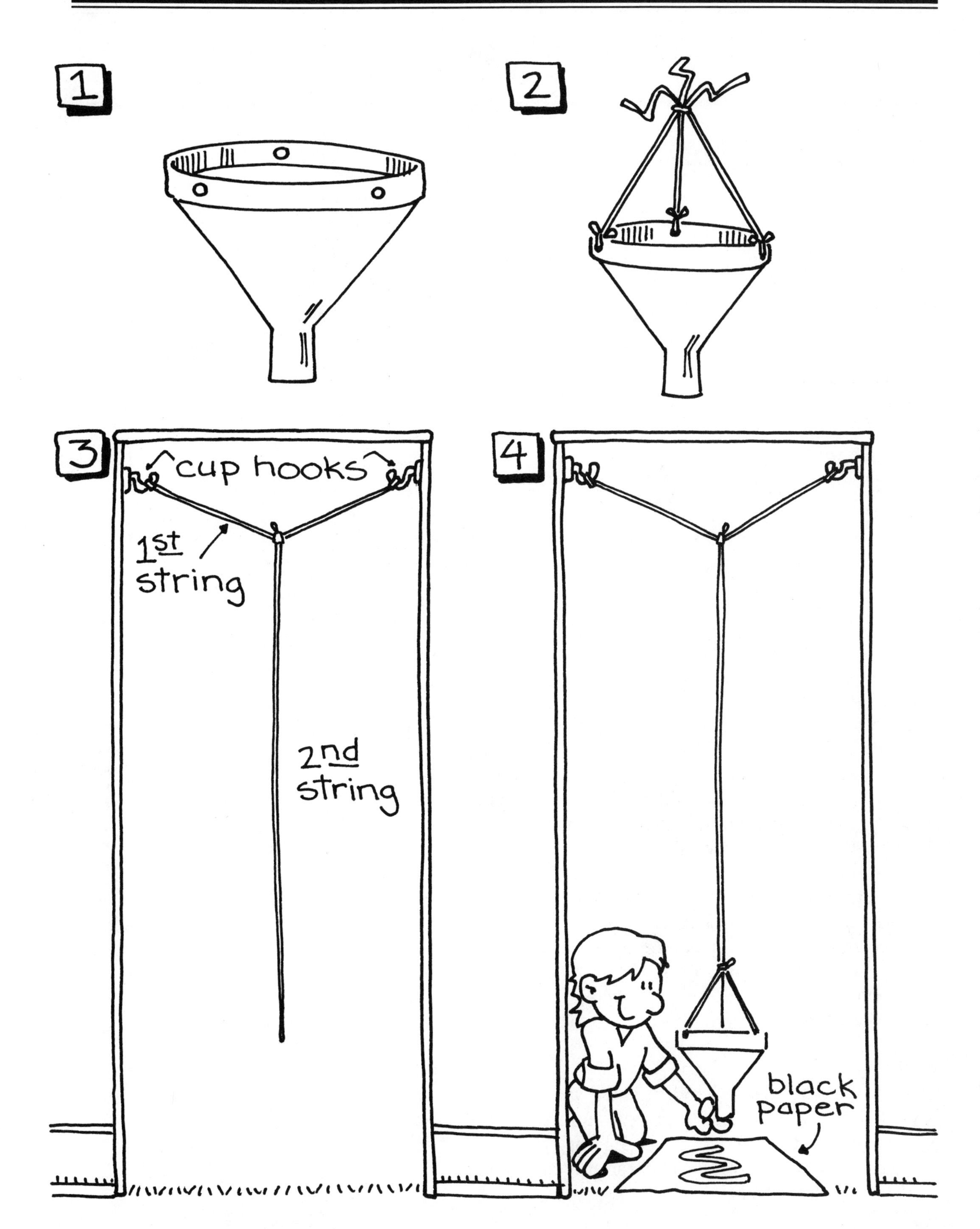
1
2
3
cup hooks
1st string
2nd string
4
black paper

Water Wheel

This activity demonstrates the power of moving water.

MATERIALS:
Styrofoam egg carton
Styrofoam packing piece
Scissors
Pencil
Large drinking straw
Four paper clips
Styrofoam cup
String

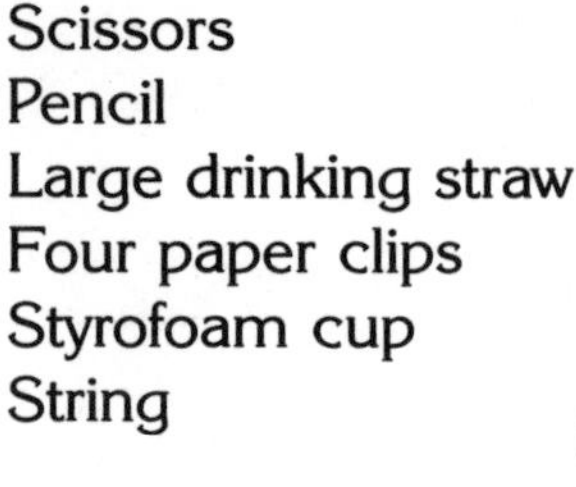

CONSTRUCTION:
1. Cut three equal strips from the egg carton lid. Cut a narrow slot halfway across the middle of each strip. Fit the strips together to form a wheel.
2. Poke a pencil through the Styrofoam packing piece, making a hole slightly larger than the diameter of the straw.
3. Cut several deep slits in one end of the straw.
4. Insert the straw into the Styrofoam block.
5. Mount the wheel onto the slotted straw end.
6. Bend each paper clip into an S-shape. Hook three clips through the lip of the Styrofoam cup. Use the fourth clip to link the free ends of the other three clips.
7. Tie one string end to the paper clip.
8. Tie the other string end through a small hole in the straw.

USE:
1. Hold the water wheel under running water. The force of the water will cause the wheel to spin, in turn moving the cup. Try to figure out how to raise and lower the cup.
2. Place a small amount of weight in the cup and see if the wheel can still move it.

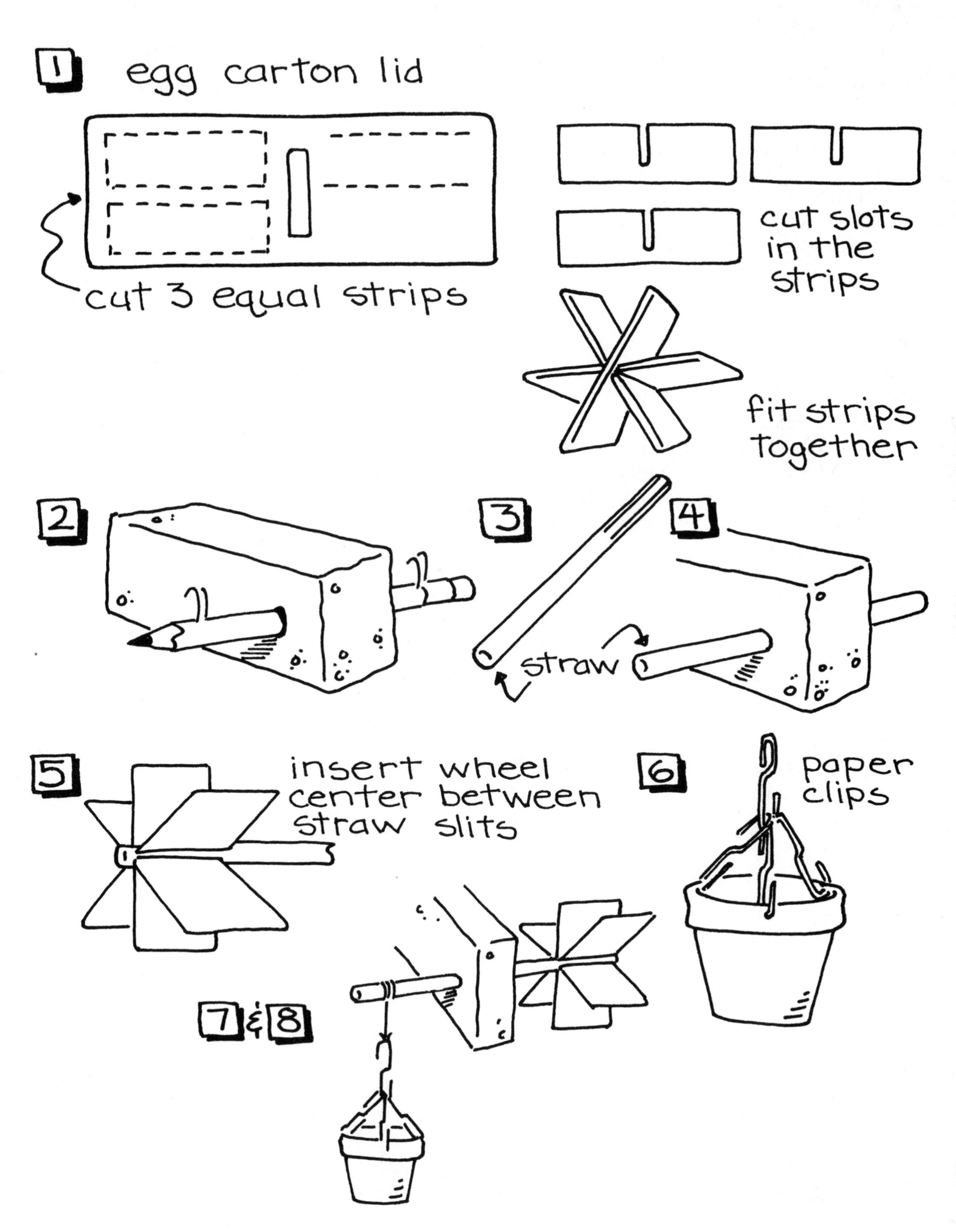
1
egg carton lid
cut 3 equal strips
cut slots in the strips
fit strips together
2
3
4
straw
5
insert wheel center between straw slits
6
paper clips
7 & 8

Merry-Go-Round Spring Toy

Energy stored in the rubber band makes this toy turn.

MATERIALS:
Large thread spool
Cotton swab or Popsicle stick
Rubber band
Paper clip
Small metal washer
Construction paper
Thread

CONSTRUCTION:
1. Hook the rubber band onto the paper clip.
2. Thread the rubber band through the hole in the thread spool. Holding on to the rubber band at the top of the spool, place the paper clip flat against the bottom of the spool.
3. At the top of the spool, push the rubber band through the washer. Insert the cotton swab or Popsicle stick through the rubber band loop.
4. Cut two small animal shapes from the construction paper.
5. Make a pin hole in the top of each shape. Push a short length of thread through each hole, and tie the animals to the end of the swab or stick.

USE:
1. Use your finger to wind the swab or stick until the rubber band feels tight.
2. Release it, and watch the merry-go-round turn.

1
paper clip
rubber band
2
rubber band
paper clip
3
rubber band
washer
4
cotton swab

Lightning Calculator

Use this instrument to determine the distance from a thunderstorm.

MATERIALS:
Paper plate
Marker
Oaktag
Scissors
Brad
Watch with second hand

CONSTRUCTION:
1. Print the numbers shown in the illustration on the paper plate.
2. Cut three arrows from the oaktag. Fasten them to the center of the plate with the brad.
3. Label the arrows 1, 2, and 3.

USE:
1. This calculator is based on the principle that sound travels about one mile in five seconds. The outer circle of numbers indicates miles. The inner circle indicates seconds.
2. During a thunderstorm, use the watch to count the seconds between a lightning flash and the sound of thunder.
3. Set the first arrow at that number of seconds. The corresponding number in the outer circle will show the distance in miles from the storm.
4. Measure another sequence of lightning and thunder, and set the second arrow. Has the storm moved closer or farther away?
5. Set the third arrow to see if the storm is continuing to move closer or farther away.

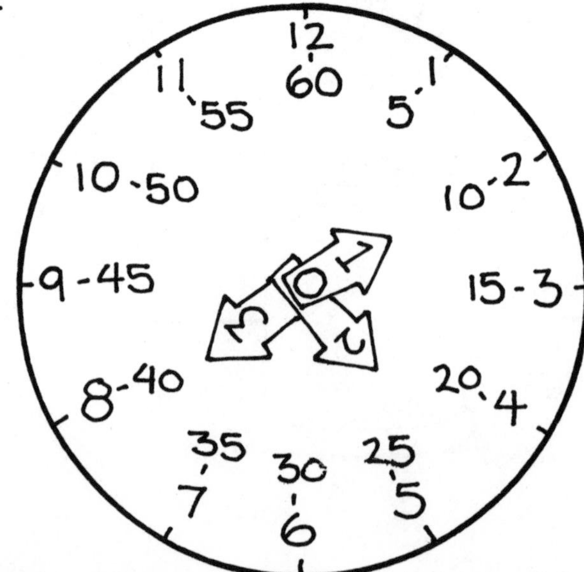

LIVING THINGS

Root View Planter

Compare the roots of three different plants in this milk carton planter.

MATERIALS:
Half-gallon milk carton
Utility knife
Plexiglas
Potting soil
Seeds of three different plants
Spray water bottle

CONSTRUCTION:
1. Cut one side from the milk carton. (Save this piece to use in step 5.) The cutout area will be the top of the planter.
2. Cut a flap on one side of the carton.
3. Measure the carton diagonally, and mark the Plexiglas to the size needed. Use a utility knife to score the lines marked. Place the Plexiglas on a table edge, and apply pressure along the scored lines to break the Plexiglas.
4. Fit the Plexiglas into the carton diagonally. (The Plexiglas is slanted so that the roots, which grow straight down, will be visible.)
5. Cut two triangular dividers to fit inside the planter.
6. Fill the three sections with potting soil.

USE:
1. Plant a different type of seed in each section, near the Plexiglas.
2. Spray the soil with water until it is damp.
3. Tape the window flap shut. (Remember that roots grow in darkness.)
4. Every few days, briefly open the window to see what's going on inside the planter. Check to see if the seeds have sprouted, noting when the roots appear and how the roots of the three types of plants differ.
5. Keep the soil slightly damp as the plants develop.

VARIATION:
Compare the growth of plants in various soils. Plant one section of the planter with potting soil, one with garden soil, and one with a mixture of sand and plant fertilizer.

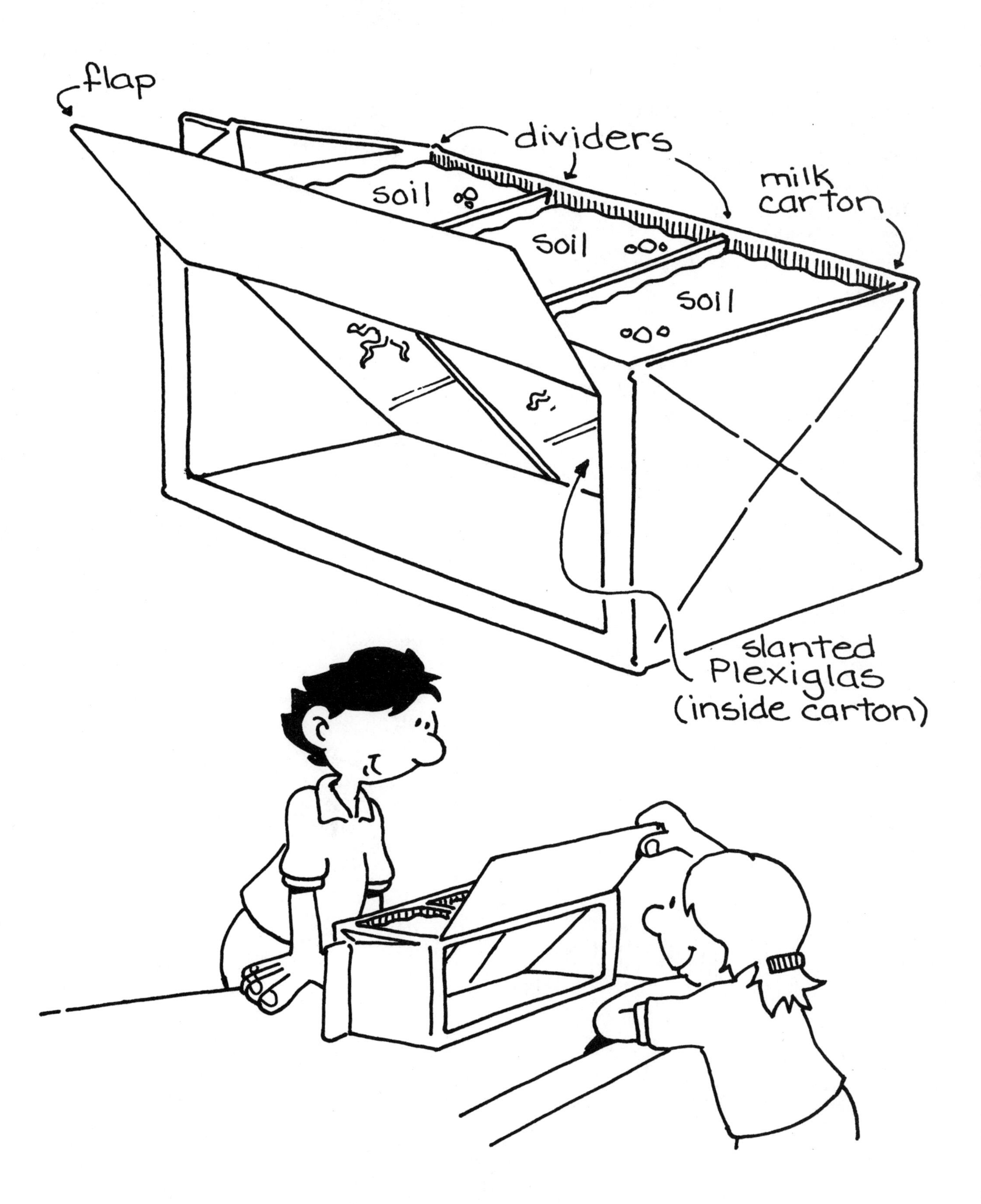
flap
dividers
milk carton
soil
soil
soil
slanted Plexiglas (inside carton)

Spicy Sprouts

Observe plant roots as they grow.

MATERIALS:
Clear jar or glass
Absorbent paper towels
Spray water bottle
Whole-seed spices or herbs (such as celery, poppy, sesame, fennel)

CONSTRUCTION:
1. Line the inside of the jar or glass with several layers of paper towels. Spray the towels with a light mist of water.
2. Place the seeds between the towels and the glass, halfway down.
3. Spray the towels with water several times a day to keep them moist.

USE:
1. Observe the growth of the seeds, and keep a record in a Science Log. Measure the lengths of the roots. Draw pictures of the seedling plants each week.
2. Begin a second sprout jar. Place it in a dark area. Compare the growth of the seedlings to the growth of the ones in the first jar.
3. Sprout different kinds of herbs or spices in different jars. Label each jar. Compare the seedlings.

Leaf Identification Cards

Make cards that match leaves on the trees outside.

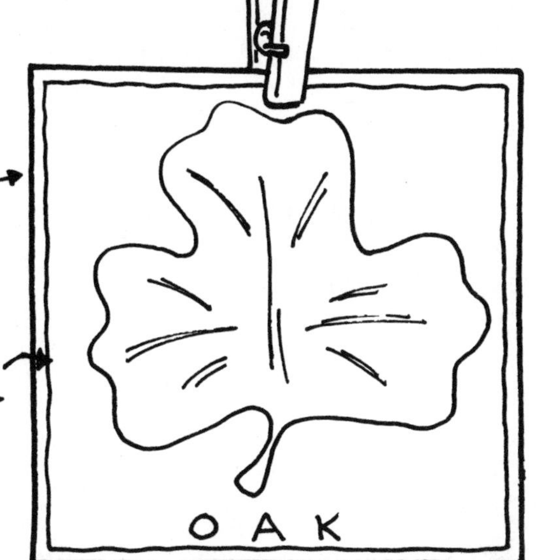

MATERIALS:
Leaves
Newspaper
Heavy book
Cardboard
Scissors
Glue
Marker
Clear adhesive paper
Clothespins

CONSTRUCTION:
1. Collect leaves from trees in the yard or neighborhood. Press the leaves between newspaper. Lay a heavy book on top of the newspaper, and allow the leaves to dry for several days.
2. Cut the cardboard into cards large enough to mount the leaves. Glue the leaves onto the cards.
3. Use an encyclopedia or other reference book to identify the leaves. Label each card with the tree name.
4. Cover the cards with clear adhesive paper.
5. Attach a clothespin to each card.

USE:
1. Challenge a group to match the Leaf Identification Cards to the trees.
2. Cards can be clipped to matching trees with clothespins.
3. Have a scavenger hunt with the cards. The winner is the person who correctly matches the most cards in the shortest length of time.

Leaf Rubbing Book

Make a collection of leaves found in the neighborhood.

MATERIALS:

Large sheet of wallpaper
Two sheets of lightweight cardboard
Glue
White typing paper
Stapler
Leaves
Crayons
Pencil

CONSTRUCTION:

1. Lay the wallpaper design-side down on a table.
2. Glue the cardboard sheets to the wallpaper, leaving a margin all the way around the edges of both pieces.
3. Fold the edges of the wallpaper over the cardboard, and glue them down.
4. Fold a sheet of typing paper in half cross-wise. Spread glue thinly on one half, and glue it to the inside front cover so that the free half stands in the middle. Repeat with another sheet of paper, gluing it to the inside back cover.
5. Fold the cover in half, creasing the spine. Then open it up again. Stack 10 to 12 sheets of paper together, and fold them evenly down the middle. Staple the pages several times along the crease.
6. Glue the first sheet of the packet of pages to the free half of paper in the front of the book. Glue the last sheet to the free half of paper in the back.

USE:

1. Place a leaf under the book page. Rub an unwrapped crayon over the page until the leaf's outline and veins are clearly visible.
2. Below the rubbing, write about the tree that the leaf came from. Use a reference book to identify the tree.
3. Fill the book with rubbings of leaves from different trees. How many different kinds are there? Do any of the different trees have leaves that look somewhat alike?

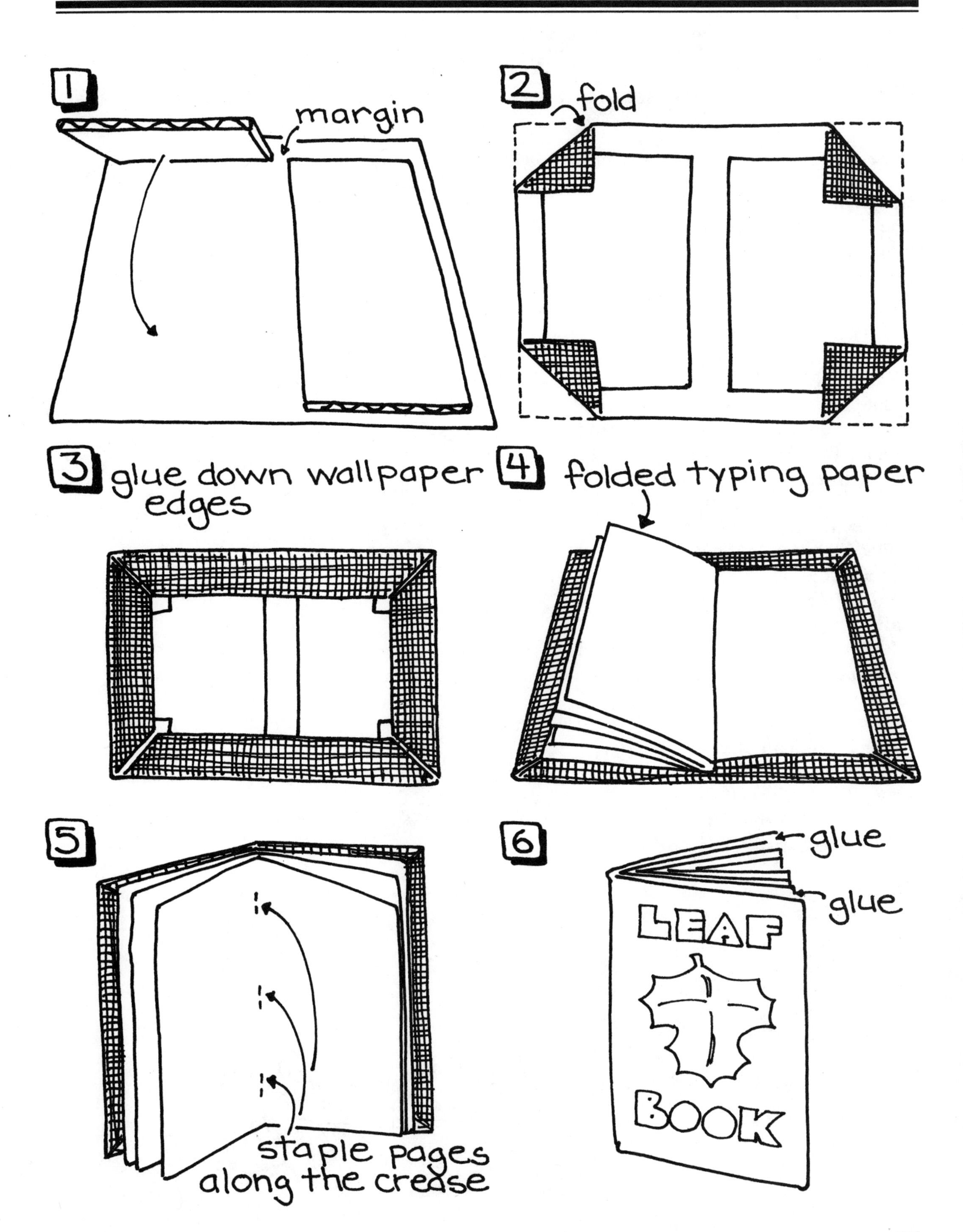
1
margin
2
fold
3
glue down wallpaper edges
4
folded typing paper
5
staple pages along the crease
6
glue
glue
LEAF
BOOK

Bird Nest Garden

Grow last year's bird nest in a mini-hothouse.

MATERIALS:
Bird nest
Kitchen tray
Spray water bottle
Clear plastic bag
Bag tie

CONSTRUCTION:
1. Late fall or winter is the best time to find an abandoned bird nest. Carefully remove the nest from its surroundings.
2. Place the nest on the tray. Take some time to examine how the nest was constructed. Check the Bird Nest Chart to try to identify the bird that built the nest.
3. Spray the nest with water until it is moist.
4. Place the tray in the plastic bag, fastening the bag above the nest with the bag tie.

USE:
1. Place the tray in a well-lighted window. The plastic bag forms a warm and moist environment, like a hothouse, that helps seeds sprout.
2. Spray the nest with water if it is dry. Watch for the appearance of green seedling plants.
3. When leaves appear, check a reference book to identify the plants. Do these plants grow in the same area as where the nest was found? Is it more likely that the seeds were carried into the nest during construction or during feeding?

Bird Nest Chart

Name	Materials	Location	Food
Bobwhite	Grass, stems, strips of bark.	On ground in grass tangles, open fields, hedgerows.	Corn, and grain. Lespedeza and weed seeds.
Field Sparrow	Coarse grasses, weeds, rootlets. Lined with fine grass and hairs.	On ground or low bushes (10 ft. or less) in fields, overgrown pastures.	Largely weed seeds, crabgrass, pigweed, sedge, etc.
Cardinal	Twigs, rootlets, strips of bark. Lined with grasses and rootlets.	In thick bushes or vines: 2-10 ft. high. Rarely up to 30 ft.	Grape, holly, blackberry; wild seeds and a good many kinds of insects.
House Wren	Twigs, stems, grasses, lined with feathers, hair.	A cavity in hollow tree: 5-60 ft. up. Woodlands, farmyards, and in cities. Bird boxes commonly used.	Small insects: beetles, caterpillars, etc.
Mockingbird	Bulky nest of coarse twigs, weed stems, shreds, string, rags.	In shrubs, thickets, vines; near houses: 1-15 ft., rarely higher.	Beetles, grasshoppers, and other insects; wild fruit in season, grape and holly *preferred.*
Robin	Mud wall and bottom, reinforced with grass, twine, twigs. Lined with grass.	In tree crotch or among branches. 5-70 ft. up. In woods or open country. On buildings, in rural areas.	Garden and field insects, worms; cultivated and wild fruits. Some seeds.
Barn Swallow	Mud reinforced with plant material. Lined with feathers.	Commonly in barns; hollows in trees, cliffs; 5-20 ft. up. Adheres to an upright surface.	Entirely flying insects: flies, bees, ants, beetles.
Blue Jay	Twigs and sticks, lined with rootlets, vines, grass.	In trees (preferably pine woods), height 10-70 ft.	Acorns, beechnuts, and other grain. Some insects, eggs, and young birds.
House Sparrow	Of any available materials: string, straw, twigs, paper, etc.	In any available place: in buildings, structures, eaves. Height: over 5 ft.	Corn, oats, wheat and other grain; weed seeds; some insects during spring and summer.
Meadowlark	Grasses and weeds; often arched over.	Usually on ground in grassy fields or meadows.	Grain and wild grass seeds, wild fruits, and insects.

Nature Rubbings

Use patterns from nature to make a picture.

MATERIALS:
Plexiglas
White glue
Toothpick
Art paper
Crayons

CONSTRUCTION:
1. Find an interesting nature object, such as a feather or a pressed flower, or use a magazine picture of an insect or an animal. Objects with simple outlines are the easiest to work with.
2. Place the object under the sheet of Plexiglas. Use white glue to trace the outline and a few details on the Plexiglas. Use a toothpick to clean the lines.
3. Allow the glue to dry for two or three days.

USE:
1. Place a sheet of art paper over the Plexiglas. Hold the paper firmly with one hand. Rub an unwrapped crayon over the paper, and watch the picture appear. Use two or three colors for a more dramatic effect.
2. Make a collection of Nature Rubbings to label and place in a Science Log.

1
magazine picture
2
Plexiglas
3
WHITE GLUE

Ant Farm

Discover how ants work to make a home in soil.

MATERIALS:
Large glass jar with metal lid
Soil
Hammer
Nail
Ants
Small sponge piece
Water
Honey, sugar, or cracker crumbs
Black construction paper
Tape

CONSTRUCTION:
1. Fill the jar with soil. Use the hammer and nail to make some air holes in the jar lid.
2. Collect a few ants (look under a rock or a log), and put them in the jar.
3. Dampen the sponge and place it on top of the soil to provide water for the ants. Mix honey or sugar with water or cracker crumbs to provide food.
4. Screw the lid on the jar.
5. Cover the jar with the black paper, taping it in place.

USE:
1. Remove the paper briefly every day to observe the ants. Are there any changes? Are there tunnels or other evidence of the ants' movements?
2. Provide moisture and food as needed.

VARIATION:
To allow the ants to leave the jar, cut a circle of cardboard to cover the jar opening. Cut a hole in the center of the cardboard. Remove the metal jar lid, and replace it with the cardboard circle. Set the jar in a dishpan of water to prevent the ants from escaping. Put a cotton ball soaked in sugar water on the cardboard to get the ants to come out of the jar.

holes
black paper
damp sponge
food
soil

Animal Tracks

Stamp tracks on paper, and then challenge someone to guess the animal!

MATERIALS:
Styrofoam meat trays
Pencil
Scissors
Thread spool
Glue
Tempera paint
White paper

CONSTRUCTION:
1. Choose an animal track from the Animal Tracks Chart. Trace the track on the back of one of the Styrofoam trays, and cut it out.
2. Glue the track onto the thread spool to make a printing stamp.

USE:
1. Mix tempera paint in another meat tray.
2. Dip the printing stamp in the paint. Then press the stamp firmly onto the paper.
3. Continue printing tracks on the paper, making them look as if the animal is walking or running.
4. See if a friend can identify the animal.

VARIATIONS:
1. Print the animal tracks on other kinds of paper, such as newsprint or wallpaper.
2. Make a poster of animal tracks, and hang it up at home or on a bulletin board at school.

Animal Tracks Chart

Deer

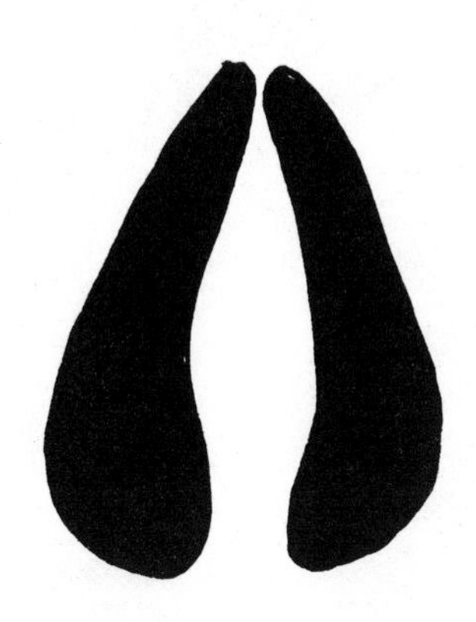

Opossum

Beaver

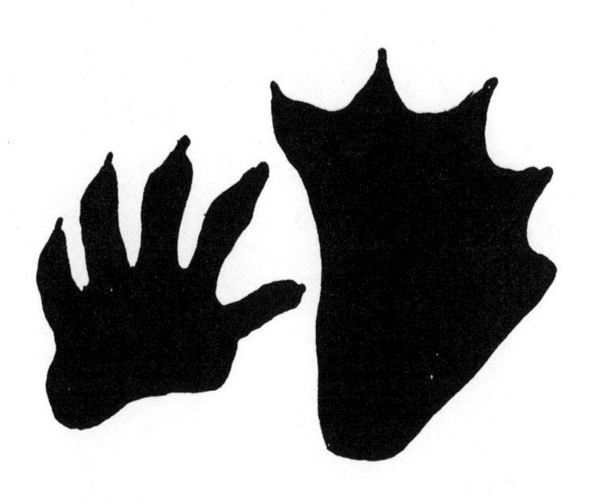

Coyote

Bison

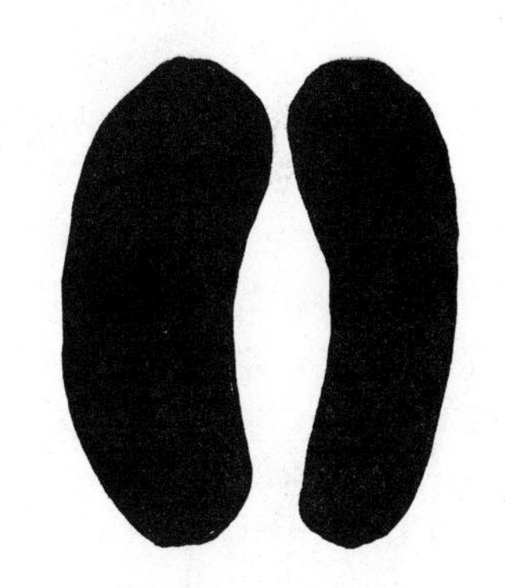

Black Bear

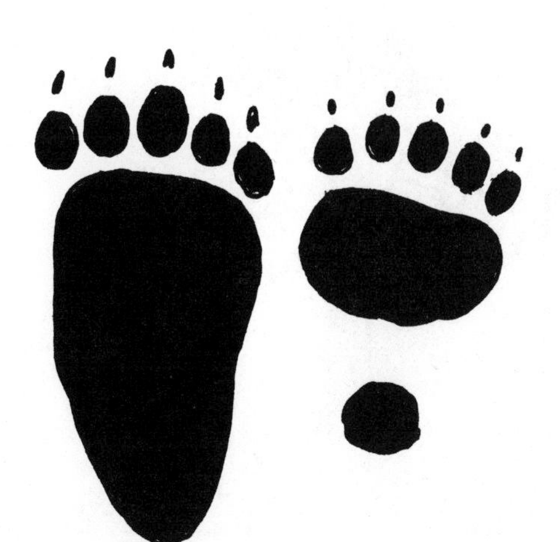

Wolf

Horse

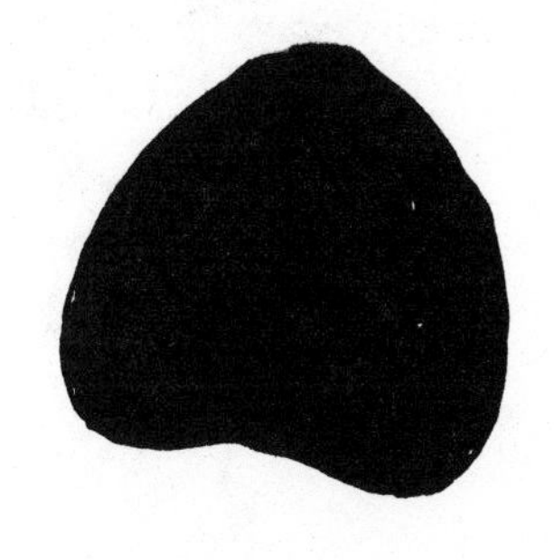

All Species Race

Try this new twist to the old relay race.

MATERIALS:
Index cards
Marker
Tape, string, or yarn

CONSTRUCTION:
1. On each index card, print the name of an animal:

rabbit	monkey	penguin
horse	dog	frog
turtle	greyhound	snake
kangaroo	duck	caterpillar
giraffe	elephant	pig

2. Mark off the beginning and the end of the race course with parallel lines of tape, string, or yarn.

USE:
1. Divide the players into two teams. Have the teams stand behind one of the lines.
2. The game leader stands behind the other line, holding the cards.
3. At the signal, the first player from each team races to the line and takes a card from the game leader. Each player reads the card, hands it back to the game leader, and races to the other line, imitating the movements of the animal on the card.
4. Each returning player tags the next team member, who races to read the next card in the deck.
5. The race continues until all team members have had a turn. The team that completes the course first wins.